MW01050093

# A Teacher's Guide to Motor Development

## Essentials for Implementing a Quality Physical Education Program for Children

**Susan Hart**

**The University of Texas at Brownsville**

KENDALL/HUNT PUBLISHING COMPANY
4050 Westmark Drive        Dubuque, Iowa 52002

*This book is dedicated to Charlie, my loving and always cheerful husband, and to my two wonderful sons, Charlie Rio and Dusty River. Their love of the outdoors and enthusiasm for life supplies my inspiration to provide opportunities for all children to experience adventure through physical activity.*

Cover art © Artville

Copyright © 2007 by Kendall/Hunt Publishing Company

ISBN 10: 978-0-7575-3967-1
ISBN 13: 0-7575-3967-X

Printed in the United States of America
10  9  8  7  6  5  4  3  2  1

# Contents

# Preface

The purpose of this text is to provide essential information for teaching physical education at the elementary school level. It is designed for use by preservice physical education teachers as well as preservice classroom teachers who may find themselves teaching and/or supplementing physical education at their elementary school. The information provided should be of interest to all individuals who are in the business of raising children. This includes school administrators (at all levels), teachers, parents, and grandparents.

The book is organized around four basic themes concerning a teacher's understanding of:
   (1) the importance of physical education for children
   (2) the effects of maturation on the ability of children to acquire motor skills and develop physical fitness
   (3) developmentally appropriate curriculum
   (4) the implementation of quality instruction

The initial chapter serves as a "wake-up call" concerning the absolute necessity for children to be afforded quality physical activity. Quintessential to teaching any subject is enthusiasm related to the importance of the material being taught to the learner. In the first chapter I have provided results from scientific research concerning the lifelong effects of physical activity and fitness behaviors during the pediatric years. This information should provide physical educators with a passion to develop quality programs, as well as classroom teachers with a strong desire to include developmentally appropriate physical activity in their pedagogy. After completing chapter 1, readers will be well equipped to advocate for quality physical education for elementary school children.

Somewhat novel to books dealing with elementary PE teaching methodology is the second section I have included in this text. While pediatric development is typically covered in college courses dealing with lifespan human development, often the information is not presented to form a connection to elementary physical education content or teaching methods. Section 2 of this text is provided as a link to understanding how many aspects of pediatric development (biological, neurological, and perceptual) impact the ability for students to learn and acquire psychomotor skills.

The 3rd section addresses how teachers can optimize course content and teaching methods for the developing child. The focus is on developing and implementing curriculum to educate the "total child," with an emphasis on building the fundamental foundation for a lifetime of physical activity. The importance of family involvement is also stressed. Research suggests that developing behavioral patterns of activity with significant others and family members is vital to ensuring an active lifestyle long after the elementary school years.

The last section supplies preservice teachers with strategies and information conducive to developing an environment optimal for student learning and safety. Although brief in content, liability and legal issues are also discussed in this section. It is very important that teachers understand what is meant by *duty*, *proper care of students*, and *negligence*. Content included in this section is designed to help novel teachers foresee potential hazards, and create safe supervised environments as well as implement safe daily lessons.

Finally, within the Appendices I have placed homework assignment examples which may be useful as teachers prepare activity lessons.

# Chapter 1
# Understanding the Necessity of Quality Physical Education during the Developmental Years

*"Exercise and recreation are as necessary as reading. I will say rather more necessary because health is worth more than learning."*
Thomas Jefferson

It is very easy to argue that Physical Education is one of the most important subjects students take at the elementary school level, yet its importance is often overlooked by school administrators, classroom teacher, parents, and even athletic coaches. In addition, too often even physical education teachers are unaware of the important and unique role of their subject to the optimal physiological, psychomotor, affective, and cognitive development of young children. This chapter is designed to empower physical education teachers, as well classroom teachers who provide physical education, with the knowledge necessary to advocate for daily quality physical education for preadolescent children.

Quintessential to advocacy is an understanding of just exactly what a quality physical education program is. Physical Education provides a unique curriculum in an array of academic subjects, in which physical fitness, motor skills, health concepts, wellness concepts, socialization, etiquette, and critical thinking are taught primarily through physical activity. In addition physical education activities are often utilized to reinforce topics covered in other disciplines such as language arts, science or math. It is a unique subject in that, if it were eliminated from the total curriculum, many of the concepts taught (directly and indirectly) would not be covered elsewhere in the child's total curriculum.

A quality physical education program is also unique in that it provides health-related physical fitness activities on a daily basis. In addition to enhancing one's quality of life from a physiological as well as a psychological perspective, the general consensus among researchers is that students who engage regularly in vigorous physical activity actually perform better in their academic subjects.

Appropriate exercise bouts have also been shown to improve the behavior of certain populations of students. For example, research suggests that aerobic exercise may help to reduce some of the behavioral problems often associate with autism and attention deficit hyper activity disorder (ADHD).

At the pre-school and elementary level, quality physical education takes on an even *greater role* in optimizing the physiological development of children. As you will discover in this chapter, exercise is *vital* during particular "critical" periods of child development. Physical educators of young children should understand their role in potentiating the physical and motoric possibilities of their students. Conversely, it's important for teachers to understand the implication of a poor physical education program.

## Focus of Early Childhood and Elementary School Physical Education: Building the Foundation for an Active Lifestyle

The ultimate goal of physical education at the elementary school level is to provide children with the physiological basis, motor skills and intrinsic desire to lead a healthy and active lifestyle. Appropriate physical activity is especially important during early childhood and the elementary years because of issues related to critical and sensitive periods of human physical and neurological development. In addition, fun and success in physical activity during these developmental years is important in creating individuals who seek out physical opportunities and challenges.

Building this foundation requires enjoyable and developmentally appropriate curriculum which focuses on two distinct areas of physical fitness: *Health Related* and *Skill-Related*.

### Components of Health-Related Physical Fitness
- Cardiovascular Endurance
- Muscular Strength
- Muscular Endurance
- Flexibility
- Body Composition

## Components of Skill-Related Physical Fitness
- Coordination
- Balance
- Agility
- Speed
- Power
- Reaction Time

# Justification for the importance of Health-Related Physical Fitness

Optimizing the health-related components of physical fitness during the elementary years is important from many different perspectives including physiological benefits, psychological benefits, and indirect benefits effecting quality of life.

## Physiological Importance

While much research has been done linking the positive effects of exercise on adult health and wellness, much of the information regarding the link between pediatric physical activity patterns and health is still quite speculative. For example, regardless of activity patterns or obesity issues, pediatric populations typically do not suffer from heart attacks due to arterial blockage, or bone fractures from osteoporosis. These are still health issues associated with adults, not children. However, a growing area of interest is in understanding the link between pediatric fitness and subsequent health during the adult years. Knowledge about the developmental aspects of specific biological systems, as well as knowledge concerning the development of chronic diseases associated with adults seems to strongly support the notion that regular physical activity and the maintenance of physical fitness is imperative during the developmental years. In support of this line of reasoning are the selected facts regarding human development:

1. The primary growth and development of the skeletal structure takes place during childhood and adolescences. Maximizing the bone density at this time may help to prevent osteoporosis during the senior years.
2. Fat accumulation during childhood takes place through an increase in the size of the cells (hypertrophy) as well as an increase in the number of fat cells (hyperplasia). During adulthood fat is gained almost exclusively through an increase in the size of the cells which were developed as a preadolescent.

3. High blood pressure, symptoms of which are generally associated with adults, often has its beginnings during later childhood and adolescents.
4. The fatty lesions on the walls of the coronary arteries which denote the precursor of atherosclerosis are generally established by the teenage years.
5. By the age of about 8 years, the number of alveoli (about 300 million) has been established. These little air sacs, required for metabolic respiration, will increase in size as the child grows to adulthood, but the number will stay constant.
6. Although an indirect advantage of exercise, vigorous activity is associated with better sleep patterns. Growth hormone, required for optimal physical growth, is produced by the pituitary gland during periods of deep sleep!

*For more information see Oded Bar-Or and Thomas W. Rowland, Pediatric Exercise Medicine, Human Kinetics (2004).*

Health-Related Statistics

Health-Related statistics also support the need for the establishment of a daily fitness component in elementary physical education. Some examples include:

- Poor diet and inadequate physical activity are the second leading cause of death in the United States and together account for at least 300,000 deaths each year. According to the Surgeon General's *Call to Action to Prevent and Decrease Overweight and Obesity* (2001) this problem has "reached epidemic proportions in the United States."

- According to the Surgeon General's report, the number of overweight children has doubled and the number of overweight adolescents has tripled since 1980.

- The CDC warns that one in three U.S. children born in 2000 will become diabetic unless they start exercising more and eating less.

- There was a 10-fold increase in the incidence of Type 2 diabetes among adolescents between 1982 and 1994 (Pinhas-Harniel, O., 1996).

- U.S. Secretary of Health and Human Services has stated that the key to fighting cardiovascular disease, cancer, Type 2 diabetes, and other chronic diseases is through prevention, which includes helping students to be physically active.

- According to researchers at the International Life Sciences Institute, fewer than 1 in 4 children get 20 minutes of vigorous physical activity per day.

- The CDC reports that as children get older their participation in all types of physical activity declines, to the extent that nearly half of America's teenagers are not physically (vigorously active) on a regular basis, and over one-third of 12 – 17 year olds are physically active less than 3 days a week .

- The CDC warns that we may be seeing the first generation of children that will not outlive their parents!

*For more statistics visit your local state health department , the Center of Disease Control (CDC) website, or see Action for Healthy Kids (http://www.Action For Healthy Kids.org)*

**Psychological Importance**
- Children who are more fit generally have greater self-confidence and self-esteem.
- Participation in rigorous physical activity reduces stress.
- Participation in regular physical activity is associated with improvements in sleep patterns.
- Participation in regular vigorous activity has been associated with a reduction in childhood depression.
- Vigorous activity increases the amount of oxygen delivered to the brain.
- Most children enjoy regular physical activity, especially when participating with friends.
- Children develop friendships through active participation with other children.

**Other Benefits of Health-Related Physical Fitness**
- Fit children typically recover from illness faster than their unfit peers.
- Children who participate in regular vigorous activity perform better in school.

- Exercise is generally suggested for children with conditions like asthma, and diabetes.
- Regular vigorous exercise has been shown to reduce the incidence of inappropriate behaviors associated with conditions such as ADHD and Autism.

## Justification for the importance of Skill-Related Physical Fitness

The development of fundamental motor skills, as well as spatial and rhythmical awareness is essential to the performance of more complex motor tasks and sport skills. That is, students who possess basic abilities such as running, jumping, climbing, throwing and catching can better adapt to novel motor tasks as various aspects of the task demand it. In addition, students who are proficient as well as confident in their basic skills are more likely to participate in organized activities as well as free play with their peers. Confident students are also more likely to seek out activity and physical challenges. Another important aspect of motor skill confidence is its relation to childhood depression, the details of which are beyond the scope of this text. To this extent it is imperative that physical educators understand the importance of skill development as they design their physical education course curriculum. Justification for the focus on developmental skills, rather than sport skills, at the elementary level include evidence from neurophysiology as well as psychological considerations.

### Neurophysiological Considerations

Findings from research suggest that early foundations of motor behavior are critical. In fact, there may be time limits, or "windows of opportunity" for optimizing neural circuits for specific behaviors, including motor skill acquisition. In theory, a lack of early affordances for skill development may result in a delayed acquisition of specific skills, and/or increased difficulty in developing these skills.

The term **affordances** refers to the availability of experiences, in this case physical movement and skill development. Modern neuroimaging techniques which enable the visualization of brain activity and the dynamics (changing) of brain structure provide solid evidence regarding the importance of early experience.

To better understand the connection between physical activity and brain development, a minimal understanding of neurodevelopmental physiology is required. The contemporary perspective is that we are born with approximately 100 billion neurons. This is perhaps a time of our greatest potential! Many scientists believe that the basic physiological and behavioral functions are "pre-wired" for immediate infant survival, but other cortical cells require stimulation (usage), without which they will soon be eliminated. In essence, we are born with functional neural circuits for respiration, cardiac function, and reflexes, but abilities like motor control and language require appropriate stimulation and result in postnatal neuroanatomical change. This ability of the central nervous system to adapt its circuitry in response to training is referred to as *neural plasticity*. In essence human babies are not born totally "prewired." The trillions of finer connections in the brain require postnatal stimulation. One advantage of plasticity is the potential it provides for treating neural disorders if they are discovered within the window of cerebral malleability. A disadvantage lies in the problems that can occur if environmental conditions are not optimal for neural development during this critical time period.

Does this suggest that students who were not afforded opportunities for motor skill development at an early age cannot learn skills later in life. Not exactly, but it does suggest that children who missed these opportunities may have a more difficult time acquiring motor skills as older children, as adolescents, and as adults. An antidotal example would be the ease at which language is learned (even learning multiple languages) before the age of three, versus the difficulty one experiences after this age. In fact it has been shown that cortical areas subserving language will be different for languages learned after the age of about 3 years. This illustrates the concept of specific window closure.

From a neurophysiological perspective, affordances during infancy and the toddler years may be of primary importance regarding neural circuit adaptation; however, research is unclear regarding the timetable of window closure for specific motor functions. In fact there is evidence to suggest that general window closure may not occur until the age of about 10 years. This is the time when neural "pruning" replaces neural proliferation (in essence, if you haven't used it you lose it)! The implication, then, is for teachers to understand the importance of teaching basic motor skills at an early age. Although currently unclear, the lack of appropriate practice during the early school years may even create a neurological disadvantage for motor skill development.

**Psychological Considerations**
- Children with proficient motor skills are typically more confident in physical education class. This confidence has potential of transferring into a generalized improvement in self-confidence (possibly across the curriculum).

- Children with confidence in motor skills are more likely to seek out physical challenges.
- Proficiency in fundamental movement skills increases the likelihood of success in novel endeavors.
- Development of fundamental motor skills and confidence in abilities in the psychomotor domain will increase the likelihood of an active lifestyle, perhaps into the adult years.

# Chapter 2
# Biological Development and Motor Ability

## Heredity

While genetic inheritance influences many visible characteristics such as eye and hair color, children also inherit a timetable regarding *rates* of physical growth, as well as neural maturation. Therefore, due to genetic makeup, some children will develop a potential for skilled coordinated movements sooner than other children of the same age. It is important to understand that individual development patterns are not determined by genetics alone. Beginning with prenatal development, the environment interacts with inherited factors to shape the physical and cognitive development of children. In essence, early experiences can actually affect the neural structure of a developing organism. This *nature-nurture* relationship will be discussed at great length as we progress through this chapter.

## Neurological Changes

A neuron (nerve cell) is the basic structural unit if the nervous system. Neurons relay information, in the form of electrochemical messages, from one cell to another through a very precise network. Some of this network is functional at birth, supporting things such as breathing, heart rate, and basic reflexes; however, experiences after birth also greatly influence the development of the neural architecture. The nervous system is divided into two parts based on function. One part of the nervous system, the Central Nervous System (CNS), is responsible for making decisions based on sensory information received from the body's internal and external environment. This "executive center" is composed of the brain and spinal cord. The neural network making up the lines of communication between the sensory organs, the muscles, and the glands is called the Peripheral Nervous System (PNS), because it is peripheral to the CNS. Within the PNS, *afferent* neurons carry information from the sensory receptors to the CNS, while *efferent* neurons carry information from the CNS to the effector organs (muscles and glands). Because of their function, afferent neurons are also referred to as *sensory* neurons, and the efferent neurons which terminate on muscle are called *motoneurons*. Over 95% of all neurons are classified as interneuron's, meaning that they originate and terminate within the CNS.

Neurons are very complex, typically connecting with thousands of other cells. In terms of structure neurons contain 3 basic parts. The *soma,* or cell body, is the metabolic center containing the nucleus and regulating basic cell processes. Extending from the soma are nerve fibers called *dendrites.* Dendrites are the receiving part of the neuron, sending messages (electrochemical signals) toward the cell body. The *axon* carries signals away from the cell body to other cells.

Cell Proliferation and Integration

The first appearance of neurons in the brain is evident during the second prenatal month. From this time until birth, neurons proliferate (increase in number) culminating in a genesis of about 100 billion. At birth almost all neuron proliferation is completed. The circuitry for basic survival functions like breathing, heartbeat, and reflexes appears to be "hardwired" at this time, but appropriate stimulation from the environment is needed to complete (and perhaps optimize) the brains neural architecture. While this period of cerebral plasticity (neural malleability), can be advantageous to human babies in terms of potential, it can also be problematic if unfortunate conditions occur. Further, in must be realized that this period of plasticity marking great potential, is short lived. The "windows of opportunity" for optimizing neural circuitry slowly close with each year of advancing age. While exact ages for window closure regarding specific functions has yet to be verified, neural pruning appears to take the place of neuronal growth at about the age of 10 years. This marks a time when neurons that have not frequently been used are eliminated.

In essence, while genetics play a major role in determining the main neural circuits of the brain, as well as the timeline of developmental events, appropriate stimulation significantly influences the finer connections that are developed after birth, and appear to strengthen the connections making them resistant to neural pruning.

Factors Effecting Neural Efficiency

Myelin is a fatty material that forms a sheath around the axons of neurons within both the CNS and PNS. The presence of myelin around axons results in faster transmission times, as well as an increase in the ability of neurons to fire repetitively with less fatigue than unmyelinated neurons.

The development of myelin is crucial to the acquisition of motor skills and continues to develop, according to a genetic timetable, throughout childhood. The development of myelin can affect the ability to visually track a moving object as well as the ability to intercept or catch a ball.

The development of myelin also affects the skill related components of physical fitness such as coordination, agility, balance, speed, power, and reaction/response time.

## Development of Selected Brain Structures
### Cerebral Lobe Development

The cerebral lobes develop at varying rates. They seem to have the following consistent order of increasing maturity.

1. Occipital Lobe- The first to mature. This lobe is associated with visual functions.
2. Parietal Lobe- The nest to mature. This lobe is primarily responsible for somatosenosry functions. That is, *kinesthetic perception* derived from the *proprioceptors*, as well as *cutaneous perception* derived from receptor organs located in the skin.
3. Temporal Lobe- The third lobe to develop. It is associated with auditory and memory functions.
4. Frontal Lobe- The slowest to develop, this lobe is responsible for motor and memory function.

Some basic understandings of how the brain develops can be helpful in terms of determining modes of presenting material to young children. For example, through neuroimaging techniques scientists concur that the occipital lobe is the first to develop. Perhaps, among other reasons suggested in subsequent chapters, this is why young children are very visual learners.

## Brain Lateralization

The two cerebral hemispheres of the brain look very symmetrical, but their functions are indeed quite different. In fact the left hemisphere is appears to control activities such as language, logic, and sequential processing. The right hemisphere seems to be more specialized for nonverbal, visuospatial functions. In terms of motor behavior, each cerebral hemisphere appears to control muscular activity in, and receive sensory input from, the opposite side of the body. Connecting these hemispheres is a tough myelinated tissue structure called the corpus collosum. Its main function is to integrate the two cerebral hemispheres. Its maturation, therefore, is essential for the development of motor asymmetries. In essence, hand preference is a result of a well developed corpus collosum. Due to the maturation of the Corpus Callosum and practice, by the age of about 4 or 5 most children have developed a lateral preference for specific activities. A Lack of preference for a limb for a specific activity (in conjunction with poor skill), may be indicative of delayed development regarding this cerebral structure (and perhaps other cerebral functions).

### The Neuromuscular Unit and Neural Recruitment

The Neuromuscular Unit - A motoneuron and all of the muscle fibers it innervates. When the neuron fires, all of the muscle fibers associated with that neuron will contract.

Prepubescent children can experience considerable strength gains through neuromuscular adaptation. Prepubescent children will not experience muscle hypertrophy (growth) like their adult counterparts.

## Physical Growth

Potential physical growth, or a child's potential increase in physical size, is a result of heredity as is the growth timetable. Other factors associated with physical growth include nutrition, disease, exercise, and possibly sleep patterns (associate with the pituitary gland's release of growth hormone). The rate of physical growth is extremely variable throughout the elementary years, making it necessary to often group students according to physical size and ability rather than simply chronological age.

### Muscle Tissue

Because of the lack of testosterone, both young boys and young girls can only experience very minimal increases in muscle mass as the result of an exercise program, yet they will experience strength gains. Muscle mass in pediatric populations basically just increases with age. The primary gains in strength associated with pediatric exercise programs are a result of an improved ability to activate motor units. The more motor units activated, the greater the contractile force of the muscle.

### Skeletal Structure

Bones need appropriate stress and good nutrition to grow strong. Without physical exercise the bones will not be able to utilize the calcium that is so important to developing bone material. There appears to be critical periods in developing strong bones, to the extent that adults after about 30 years of age have a much more difficult time building strong dense bones. Thus children need to take advantage of the developing years for building bone mass and density.

At the ends of developing bones (also referred to as the epiphysis) there is a growth plate (epiphyseal growth plate). If this area is injured, further growth of the bone will be retarded to the extent that the bone may completely stop growing. Typically an injury to the growth plate takes place through trauma, but can also happen through overuse.

## Body Composition

A child's ratio of lean body mass to fat mass is a good indicator of physical fitness. Children gain body fat through an increase in the size of the fat cells (hypertrophy) as well as an increase in the number of fat cells (hyperplasia). After adolescents however, fat mass is gained almost exclusively by increasing the size of the cells that were accumulated during childhood. Muscle tissue, on the other hand, is quite different. We are actually born with just about all the muscle fibers we will ever have, the fibers just get larger during childhood primarily due to natural physical growth patterns, and minimally larger in response to exercise. After puberty, with an increase in the level of testosterone, muscle fibers will undergo hypertrophy as an adaptation to appropriate overload. Prior to puberty, boys and girls have just about equal amounts of testosterone, very little! Hence, their ability to gain muscle mass is minimal. After puberty, both males and females experience an increase in testosterone level, making muscle hypertrophy possible. Males will experience a much greater increase, thus their potential for muscle mass increase is much greater that for their female counterparts.

The correlation between adult obesity and childhood obesity becomes stronger and stronger the closer obese children get to adolescence. Two factors that strongly account for this correlation are physiology (an overabundance of fat cells), and bad eating and exercising habits established during the childhood years.

Body builds, or "somatotypes" are often classified using the following terminology:
Endomorph-round or pudgy, pear shaped in appearance
Ectomorph- thin, lanky
Mesomorph- muscular

For the most part, children with an endomorphic somatotype are at a disadvantage for physical activity, and for acquiring new motor skills. The additional adipose tissue makes fitness activities as well as skilled physical movement more difficult and thus demotivating.

Elementary are children with a mesomorphic somatotype have been shown to be at an advantage for physical activity and skill acquisition. Mesomorphic elementary aged children appear to have an advantage even in activities requiring long distance running.

## Anaerobic Power and Muscular Endurance

Exercise bouts which are short and intense such as resistance training, or wind sprints create a by product in the muscles called lactic acid. This substance causes muscle soreness which many adults have experienced after starting a weight training program. The muscles of children are *qualitatively* different than adults in many ways, but specifically in their ability to tolerate the presence of lactic acid. Children have a much lower threshold for lactic acid and the muscles simply cannot continue to contract in the presence of very much of this substance. Therefore, children have much less anaerobic power than adults, for qualitative reasons related to muscle biochemistry, not just the size the fact that their muscles are typically much smaller than adults.

## Cardiorespiratory Development

- Aerobic Power - Basically this refers to how well the body can take in and utilize oxygen. Although children have a lower total aerobic power than adults, when a correction is made for the size difference (kids are smaller), children actually have aerobic power that is equivalent if not slightly better than their adult counterpart.

- Stroke Volume - The amount of blood pushed through the heart per stroke. Children have a lower stroke volume than adults, primarily because they have a smaller heart muscle. This results in a higher heart rate than adults.

- Basal Metabolic Rate – A child's metabolism is much faster than an adult. Children will naturally have higher heart rates, burn calories faster and need to eat more often than adults.

## Developmental Progression

- Cephalocaudal – Growth proceeds longitudinally from the head to the feet
- Proximodistal – Growth proceeds from the center of the body toward the periphery.

- Gross to Fine – Skill acquisition generally takes place on a developmental continuum from the acquisition of gross motor skills to more fine motor control. This continuum is related to the maturation of the nervous system as well as physical practice.

## Terminology

- Motor Learning - A long-term change in the performance of a motor skill resulting from practice and/or experience.
- Motor Control – A long-term change in the performance of motor skills as a result of the maturation of the underlying biological systems involved in movement.
- Motor Development - Changes in motor skill ability as a result of the biological, and behavioral, changes associated with a developing organism.
- Growth - A change in size or quantity.
- Maturation - Qualitative changes in motor performance dependent upon a genetic timetable for motor control as well as experience and practice.
- Readiness – Level of maturation that prepares an individual to acquire a skill or understanding. Very skill and/or concept dependent.
- Adaptation- The process of altering physiology and/or behavior in order to optimize survival in a changing environment.
- Critical Period- An optimal time period for the development of specific processes and behaviors.
- Neural Recruitment- Neural adaptation.

# Chapter 3
# Perceptual Changes and Motor Development

The ability to properly receive and interpret sensory information, from the external as well as the internal environment, is essential to the learning and performance of motor tasks.

The learning and subsequent performance of skilled movement relies on the following basic elements:

*Sensation – Perception – Response Selection – Response Execution*

**Sensation-** Refers to the stimulation of sensory receptors. Sensations may be received from the external or the internal environment. Our organs of sensation are dynamic in terms of adaptation abilities and natural developmental patterns. To this extent, when dealing with children, it should not be assumed that all organs of sensation are fully developed. In fact a better assumption is that they are not yet functioning at an adult level of proficiency.

Our organs of sensation take time to develop, as does our ability to detect and attenuate to specific sensory transmissions. The continual bombardment of transmissions impacting the central nervous system necessitates the ability to selectively attend to appropriate stimuli for a specific behavior. Selective attention requires maturation and practice. Can you fully understand the lecture when your friend is whispering in your ear? Can you devote your full attention to driving your car while talking on your cell phone?

**Perception-** The interpretation of sensory information. It involves long term memory because sensations are given meaning. Sensations are organized, classified and interpreted. With limited experiences, children require time and practice to classify and interpret sensations. Children become much better at catching a baseball with a glove when they have had practice trapping and catching softer (less intimidating) balls with their body and hands because they have had time to experience ball speed, and the dynamics of a moving ball.

**Response Selection** - The determination of a response base upon available skills. The child selects a course of action based upon the current information and what alternatives he/she has developed from past experiences.

**Response Execution** - The extent to which one can successfully perform a planned movement. Although a child can process incoming information and select appropriate responses, the actual execution is also dependent upon the child's ability to perform the action that has been selected. This includes the maturation of systems required for motor control, well as practice and confidence.

## Perceptual Modalities

| | |
|---|---|
| Visual | Tactual |
| Auditory | Olfactory |
| *Kinesthetic* | Gustatory |

Most physical education teachers would agree that *vision* and *kinesthesis* are the two perceptual modalities most important to the learning of motor skills. Because of their importance to the acquisition of motor skills, information regarding the developmental sequence of these sensory modalities can be very useful as teachers of elementary age children consider optimal modes of lesson presentation.

While most classroom teachers would agree on the importance of vision related to seeing the chalkboard, computer screen, or textbook, other more dynamic features of vision are perhaps more important to children in the physical education class. For example, optimal vision is crucial for judging moving objects and predicting flight patterns as well as speed.

Because of the importance of these sensory modalities to the acquisition of motor skills, the developmental changes that occur during the elementary school years with regard to vision and kinetheses, has been included in this chapter.

Vision
* **Visual Acuity-** Clearness of vision.
    > **Static-** Clearness of vision in situations where minimal physical movement exists in the child and the object being viewed is stationary. Adult level is typically reached between 1 and 5 years.
    > **Dynamic-** Clearness of vision regarding moving objects. Adult levels are reached at about 12 years.

- **Perceptual Constancy-** Refers to the ability to recognize an objects regardless of the angle of orientation or distance. The ability to perceive that an object is a constant size, regardless of the distance from the viewer. Adult-like abilities are typically not fully attained until children are about 10 to 11 years old.
- **Spatial Orientation-** The ability to perceive the orientation of objects, boundary lines, and body parts regardless of the point of reference. Examples include the accurate perception of designated space for movement, as well as correct recognition of mirror images. More difficult aspects of spatial orientation (including right/left and mirror image reversals) do not appear to reach adult levels in most children until about the age of 8 years.
- **Figure-Ground Perception-** The ability to isolate an object from its surrounding background. This perceptual ability requires development of specific visual structures as well as selective attention and concentration abilities. Although rapid improvement takes place between ages 4 and 8, capabilities continue to improve between the ages of approximately 13 to 18 years old.
- **Depth Perception-** The ability to judge the distance of an object from one's self is referred to a absolute distance, where the ability to judge the distance between two objects is referred to a relative distance. An example of relative distance is the ability of an individual to judge which one of his teem mates is closer to the goal. Although it appears that some depth perception capabilities are present in infants, adult-like levels are not reached until about 12 years of age.
- **Peripheral Vision-** The extent of the environment that can be seen without changing the fixation of the eyes on a pre-established focal point. With the eyes fixated on a point straight ahead most adults have about a 180 degree lateral visual field, with a vertical field of vision of about 47 degrees above and .65 degrees below the midline of the focal point. While marked improvements are reached in the 5 year old, lateral peripheral vision may not peak until the age of 35!
- **Perception of Movement-** The development of saccadic eye movements, necessary for the ability to focus on and track moving objects, necessitates both muscular as well as neurological development. Most children will not reach an adult-like level of this ability until they are about 12 years old.

- **Coincident Timing-** In addition to the ability to successfully track a moving object, coincident timing also requires the ability to predict speed of movement and coordinate body movement in order to intercept the object in flight. In addition to visual perception capabilities, practice and skill are also major components in the success of coincident timing. These variables make age-related predictions very difficult.

## Kinesthetic Perception

Kinesthesia is the ability to know what movements our body is making and what position it is in, relative to the external environment, based solely on information provided from inside the body. While other sensory modalities like vision and audition receive information from the external environment, the kinesthetic system provides "body knowledge" based on sensory organs located in the inner ear, muscles, tendons, and joints. As expressed earlier in this chapter, kinesthesia in association with vision, are vital to the development of skilled movement.

- **Kinesthetic Acuity-** The ability to detect differences in characteristics of objects, as well as location of body parts. Examples include differentiating qualities such as weight, location, distance, force, speed, and acceleration.

Example: when blindfolded
  1. determine which hand is raised higher than the other
  2. determine differences in weight placed in the hands
  3. determine differences in force of impact on a body part
- **Kinesthetic Memory-** The ability to reproduce specific movements of the body (without visual cues).

Acuity improves earlier than memory. Kinesthetic acuity will typically approaches adult levels in the 8 years old, but kinesthetic memory abilities will not mature levels until about the age of 12 years.

- **Body Awareness-** Also referred to as body knowledge, body concept, or body schema. The awareness of the capabilities of various body parts and their relationship to movement. This awareness also refers to ability to name and locate various body parts which is associated with the development of verbal skills.
- **Spatial Awareness-** The general sense of exactly where the body is in relationship to the external environment. The sense space needed for mobility. Practice and instruction has been shown to result in significant improvement in spatial awareness even in preschool age children.

- **Directional Awareness**- Involves the perceptual distinction of the 2 sides of the body. Laterality is a dimension of directional awareness. It involves the independent and coordinated use of the limbs. Also associated with spatial awareness.
- **Vestibular Awareness**- Required for balance. Prerequisite to proficient postural control is the integration of anatomical and neurological functions, including the development of the skeletal, muscular, sensory, and motor systems. Vestibular awareness includes features related to both static and dynamic features of balance tasks.
- **Rhythmic Awareness**- Creating or maintaining a temporal pattern which is internally initiated or matched to an external tempo. The sense of rhythm is associated with coincident timing abilities with regard to prediction of rhythmical patterns. Great improvement in the ability to keep time (to music) between 2 & 6 years.

# Chapter 4
# Developmental Factors Effecting Motor Learning

*"Children are born intrinsically motivated to be physically active. That motivation- if kept alive by physical success, freedom, and fun will do more than promote fitness behaviors that add years to life. It will maintain the physical zest that adds life to the years."*
James Whitehead, University of North Dakota

The focus of this chapter is to provide a brief explanation of several aspects of human development that affect the ability of children to benefit from practice and past experience. The purpose for including this information is to help teachers develop optimal instructional strategies for elementary school age children. It must be understood that quality physical education involves developmentally appropriate pedagogy in three separate, but interrelated behavioral domains. That is, PE teachers are responsible for teaching "knowledge" concepts related to *cognition,* as well as appropriate behavior and peer relations involved in *psychological affect.* Let us not forget that physical educators are also responsible for improving their student's physical function in the *psychomotor* domain. This includes enhancing student's health-related fitness as well as motor skill development.

## Piaget's Theory of Cognitive Development
Perhaps one of the most influential (and accepted) efforts in understanding cognitive development can be attributed to Jean Piaget (1952, 1963, & 1985). Piaget believed that cognitive development was dependent on the interaction of biological maturation and experience. He believed that cognitive development necessitated interaction with the environment. According to the author, children are innately driven to pursue "cognitive equilibrium." As they discover their environment, children constantly reorganize their structures of thought, as well as their motor behaviors to meet ever changing environmental demands. In essence, Piaget explained cognitive development in terms of a child's constant *adaptation* to novel environmental experiences.

At the root of Piaget's theory is the notion of specific periods of development.

## Sensorimotor Period (0 – 2 years)
This period spans basic reflex behavior to the development of "schema." Schema, as explained by Piaget, is a basic organized pattern of sensorimotor function such as grasping, striking, kicking, or throwing. This period is characterized by egocentrism and trial and error learning.

## Preoperational Period (2 to 7 years)
The child begins to discover themselves and the environment through play. Children begin to use symbolic language although they really are unsure of the meaning of it. Children at this stage still do not possess the ability to understand that basic properties of objects remain unchanged even if the superficial appearance is altered. An example would be that a short wide glass can hold the same volume as a tall skinny one.

## Concrete Operations (7 to 11 years)
Children begin to think in a logical manner although their reasoning is limited to the consideration of only concrete or actual experiences. A highlight of this period is the child's ability to think from various perspectives, denoting a shift from egocentrism.

## Formal Operations (11 and older)
The adolescent is able to reason beyond the world of concrete experiences. Cognition includes logic, and systematic problem solving strategies. Hypotheses can now be formed to explain events, and children can test these hypotheses in a deductive fashion.

Piaget's writings were clear regarding the necessity of play, or "action-oriented" activities for cognitive development. The importance of play to development has also been discussed in this light by Carl Gabbard, a noted contemporary researcher of motor development. The author states "Through play, the child is given the opportunity to test novel physical, cognitive, emotional, and social patterns that cannot be accommodated in the real world, thus a buffered form of learning. Once he patterns have been tested through play, they become part of one's memory bank; hence from a cognitive perspective, play permits the development of intelligence. Play also gives the child the opportunity to practice and expand on existing knowledge."

# Memory and Motor Learning

Memory refers to the ability to retain and subsequently recall information. Memory in the psychomotor domain refers to the somewhat permanent change in psychomotor skill performance as a result of experience and/or practice.

Although many theories exist, two that appear promising and of practical importance to physical education teachers are the *Information Processing* view, and the *Dynamical Systems* perspective.

## Information Processing Model of Memory

Many researchers support idea that is memory is made up of separate memory systems. Humans are "processors," therefore humans store, code, and retrieval information similar to a computer. Unlike Piaget, many information processing enthusiasts don't consider cognitive development to be stagelike, but rather a result of quantitative, rather than qualitative, changes.

The notion of information processing suggests the following sequential processes which will be described in light of the structural and functional dynamics associated with human development.

*Sensation* – Information processing requires that information be received through the sensory system in some form or fashion. As noted in chapter 3, knowledge regarding the developmental aspects of specific sensory modalities is of great importance when delivering information to children.

*Short-Term Sensory Store*- This store appears to be limitless in capacity; however, the duration of information in this store is less than one second. In addition, information is lost as new information enters. Information in this store is literal, with no abstractions. There doesn't appear to be a difference between young children and adults regarding the initial intake of information.

*Short Term Memory*- This store is very dependent upon the ability to selectively attenuate to appropriate stimuli. The short term store can only hold about 7 to 9 "chunks" of information for about 60 seconds or less. The ability to chunk information is vital and appears to be related to individual abilities as well as strategies. Great improvements occur in STM between the ages of 3 to 7 years.

Because of the importance of selective attention abilities to Short Term Memory, the following information has been provided.

*Attention* - The "focalization and concentration of consciousness" (James, 1890)
   Important to understand that:
   1. Attention is limited- An individual capacity exists.
   2. Attention is apparently performed in a serial manner, suggesting that individuals attend to one thing and then another and it is often quite difficult (sometimes impossible) to combine certain activities (Schmidt, 1988).

Three basic concepts associated with attention and motor behavior have been identified (Schmidt, 1988, & Magill, 1993):
   1. Attention involves alertness and preparation of the motor system to produce a response. An inverted U relationship exists between Arousal and Performance, such that an optimal state of arousal results in the best performance and the best state related to attention abilities.
   2. Attention is related to an individual capacity to process information.
   3. The successful performance of a motor task requires selective attention, the ability to select and attend to meaningful information.

Divided Attention

Because capacity is believed to be limited, interference could occur if more than one activity requires the same resources.
   Interference could result in:
   1. Loss of speed or quality in the performance of one of the activities.
   2. Both activities could be affected.
   3. The second activity could be ignored.

Improvements in "multitasking" appear with age and seem to be the result of the development of cognitive processes and the ability to adopt strategies. Some researchers also believe that improvement may be the result of structural increases in terms of neural adaptation.

Three Stages of Selective Attention (Ross, 1976)
   1. The Overexclusive Mode of Selective Attention is associated with children 2 to 5 years old. At this age children most often pay exclusive attention to one stimuli in a display (often at the expense of relative information), but are more easily distracted than older children.

2. The Overinclusive Mode of Selective Attention is associated with children 6 to 11 years old. This age child will typically attend to several features in a display, many of which are irrelevant.
3. Selective Attention usually develops by early adolescence. At this age individuals are capable of attending to relevant stimuli in displays of varying complexity.

A research finding that is of importance to physical education teachers is the attenuation problems that may occur when providing auditory stimulation while teaching using visual cues. In fact it appears that when auditory and visual stimuli are presented simultaneously, children up the age 12 seem to attend to auditory stimuli, to the extent that they become distracted form key visual information. Teaching Implication- Turn off the music when teaching!

*Long Term Memory*- The storage capacity and duration are seemingly unlimited. Children develop rehearsal ability at about 7 to 8 years of age, and chunking strategies greatly improve in 9 to 10 year olds.

*Recall*- The ability to retrieve information appears to be very dependent upon processing strategies used when information was learned and/or remembered. Teachers play a vital role in facilitating the ability of students to recall information.

*Most researchers agree that developmental differences in memory abilities are primarily a result of processing strategies, rather than structural (capacity) increases.*

## Dynamic Systems Perspective
This approach to the study of motor skill development is a multidisciplinary effort to explain how a system or particular action evolves with age and experience. Central to the theory is that no single central controlling devise exists. Instead, the development of motor skills and the rate of skill development is a result of the development of subsystems including the neurological system, muscular system, skeletal system, etc.

# Chapter 5
# The Objectives of Physical Education

*"To live is to move. Movement gives expression to letters and digits and sounds that to children, in an academic setting, may have no meaning."*
*Robert Sylvester, Oregon State University*

Guidelines for implementing a quality physical program can be obtained through The National Association for Sport and Physical Education (NASPE). This organization, consisting of leaders in the field of physical education, has created a number of documents to assist physical education teachers in developing and implementing, as well as advocating for quality physical education programs. In addition, this organization has developed National Standards for Physical Education (K – 12), which along with their respective benchmarks, constitutes the framework for a quality program curriculum. See *Moving into the Future, National Standards for Physical Education* (McGraw-Hill, 2004). These standards promote skill competency, knowledge, regular participation, physical fitness, and the development of social skills and lifelong activity patterns. These standards do not support the implementation of a strict sports model for quality physical education.

## <u>Philosophy</u>

The quality physical education program is designed to educate the "total child." The purpose of physical education is to help each child reach his or her potential primarily through movement experiences. There is general agreement that educating the "total" child necessitates addressing the development of three separate, but interrelated behavioral domains. These domains are:

- **Psychomotor** - Refers to the development of motor skills.
- **Physical Fitness** - Often included as a component of the psychomotor domain, physical fitness refers to the optimal functioning of the body.
- **Affective**- Learning in this domain refers to the development of positive attitudes and behaviors. Through developmentally appropriate physical activity children can develop self-esteem, self-confidence, and self-discipline. In addition, appropriate teaching can facilitate the development of social skills such as cooperation, sharing, leading, and supporting.

- **Cognitive**- Cognition refers to the development of knowledge related to motor skills, physical fitness, game rules and strategy, etc. In addition activities in PE can strengthen concepts learned in other academic disciplines. Cognitive learning also includes: understanding and communicating concepts and ideas, problem solving, critical thinking, vocabulary, and creativity. As noted in chapter 4, Jean Piaget, one of the most renowned child psychologists of our time, contends that children develop cognitive abilities through movement activities and exploring their environment.

## Teaching Fundamental Skills and Developing Fitness versus the Sports Model Approach

The information provided in the first 4 chapters of this text attest to the importance, from a developmental perspective, of a quality physical education program for elementary school children. Because of the importance of the development of fundamental motor skills and the necessity of physical fitness during childhood, a strict sports model approach to curriculum is not advocated for at the elementary school level.

A traditional sports model approach to physical education includes the development of a selected number of sport units, typically reflecting traditional sports like basketball, softball, volleyball, kickball, etc. The activities taught are limited to developing skills specific to performance in the selected sport. While sport skill development is a positive outcome of a physical education program, this approach is limiting regarding behavioral and skill related outcomes that may be required for confident participation in a greater variety of activities that may be encountered on the playground or later in life. In addition, such a curriculum may fall short in developing the skills and motivation necessary for lifelong participation in activity.

The more contemporary perspective is that a quality elementary school physical education should be designed to develop motor skills, physical fitness, movement awareness and competence, knowledge, and psychological affect that will transcend a variety of endeavors including, but not exclusive to sport skills. The curriculum should include activities for a developmentally divers group of students within each grade level classification so that learning is optimized on an individual child basis. In addition, children should learn a variety of games, dances, etc. that are fun and motivating and encourage lifetime participation. Children should learn how to modify games and create activities that can be played with peers outside of class time. Competitive sports, as well as individual challenges and cooperative games should be included in the curriculum. In addition, children should be encouraged to include family member participation in a variety of activities taught in class which promote a healthy and active lifestyle.

## Psychomotor Fitness
Fundamental Movement Skills and Movement Awareness
The fundamental movement skills necessary for most physical activities can be categorized as the following:
- *Fundamental Locomotor Skills*: Walking, Running, Leaping, Jumping, Hopping, Galloping, Sliding, Skipping, Body Rolling, and Climbing.
- *Fundamental Nonlocomotor Skills*: Dodging, Stretching & Bending, Turning & Twisting, Pushing & Pulling, Swinging & Swaying.
- *Manipulative Skills*: Ball Rolling, Throwing, Bouncing & Dribbling, Striking, and Kicking.
- *Movement Awareness*: Body & Spatial Awareness, Directional Awareness, Temporal/Rhythmical Awareness, Vestibular Awareness, Tactile and Auditory Awareness.
-

Essential to proficient fundamental movement are the components of *Skill Related Fitness.*
- *Agility*- The ability to efficiently change direction or body position.
- *Coordination*- The ability to integrate motor and perceptual systems.
- *Balance*- The ability to maintain equilibrium while moving or remaining in a stationary position,
- *Power*- The ability to transfer energy explosively into force. Includes the components of speed and force.
- *Speed*- The ability to perform movements in a short period of time.
- *Reaction Time*- The time between the onset of a stimulus and the initiation of a response. Thought to be primarily innate, not much improvement with practice.

## Health Related Physical Fitness
Physical conditioning that provides resistance from diseases associated with a sedentary lifestyle is referred to as *health-related fitness*. Research suggests that health-related physical fitness can be improved and maintained through regular and moderate physical activity.

Components of Health Related Physical Fitness:

- *Cardiovascular Fitness-* The ability of the heart, blood vessels, and the respiratory system to deliver oxygen efficiently during prolonged exercise.
- *Muscular Strength-* The ability of the muscles to exert force.
- *Muscular Endurance-* The ability to exert force with the skeletal muscles during prolonged exercise.
- *Flexibility-* The range of motion through which a joint can move.
- *Body Composition-* The proportion of fat mass to lean body mass.

## Affective Objectives of Elementary School Physical Education

- Positive Self-Esteem and Self-Concept
- Self-Management and Self-Discipline
- Socialization Skills including
  - Cooperation Skills
  - Leading
  - Providing Group Support from a Non-Leadership Position
  - Playing by the Rules
  - Playing Fair

## Cognitive Objectives of Elementary School Physical Education

- Critical Thinking
- Effective Communication
- Rules and Strategies of a Variety of Games
- Ability to Create Games
- Knowledge of the Importance of a Healthy Active Lifestyle
- Knowledge Related to Different Modes/Forms and Principles of Exercise
- Knowledge Related to Eating and Nutrition
- The Ability to Differentiate between Physical Fitness and Physical Activity
- Reinforcement of Concepts Learned in other Academic Disciplines

# Chapter 6
# Guidelines for Developing Physical Fitness

The physical fitness curriculum should be designed to develop and maintain *health-related physical fitness*. Curriculum should be appropriate for the age and fitness level of each student. It is important that activities are non-threatening, yet challenging, creating a motivating and non-intimidating environment for students.

A *health-related physical fitness* should focus on activities designed to improve aspects of physiological function that offer an optimal quality of life, including ease of movement and motor function, and decreased risk diseases which result from a sedentary lifestyle. *Performance related physical fitness* programs are designed to enhance physical ability related to the performance of a specific athletic endeavor. This type of program should <u>not</u> be included in the general physical education curriculum.

In addition to a wealth of position papers on physical activity for children, NASPE has also developed general guidelines regarding the intensity, frequency, and duration of age appropriate physical activity. Basically NASPE suggests that children accumulate between 60 minutes to several hours of appropriate physical activity on all or most days of the week. While the majority of exercise should be intermittent, bouts of activity lasting 15 minutes or more each day is also suggested. In addition, and perhaps integral to the NASPE guidelines is the position that children should not have extended periods, lasting two or more hours, of inactivity during the daytime.

## Cardiovascular Fitness

Improvements in the function of the heart, lungs, and vasculature result from the body's remarkable ability to adapt to an exercise program which regularly taxes these systems. In addition, aerobic exercise is a great way to improve body composition.

Specific guidelines for cardiovascular exercise are dependent upon the developmental level of the child. Activities will vary, based upon the physiological maturation as well as on the development of motor skills. While jumping rope may be a good cardiovascular activity for a skilled 5th grader, it would not be a good cardiovascular activity for a kindergarten student who does not have the skills to jump rope.

As teachers develop age appropriate cardiovascular exercise programs for their students, factors such as *frequency, intensity* and *duration* should be considered.

- Frequency- Children at the elementary school level should exercise everyday, or at least most days of the week.
- Intensity- Children naturally have higher resting heart rates than their adult counterparts. Healthy resting heart rates for children can range from 60 to 90 beats per minute. This higher heart rate makes up for children's lower stroke volume (resulting from naturally smaller hearts). During intense exercise, a child's heart rate can speed to 200 beats per minute. While research on adults suggests an optimal exercise intensity of about 60% to 80% of maximal heart rate for cardiovascular fitness activities, currently there is very little research to predict an optimal training intensity for cardiovascular improvement in preadolescent children.
- Optimal duration of cardiovascular activities for adult populations appears to be somewhere between 20 and 45 minutes. Recommendations regarding the duration of continuous and repetitive activities to build cardiovascular fitness is substantially less for children and is very dependent upon age and motivation.
- Progression- It is important to start easy and progress slowly. Starting students with too difficult a program can be extremely discouraging.

Practical Implication

From a practical perspective, it is suggested that young students regularly engage in bouts of exercise that elevate both heart and respiratory rates. With practice, children can learn to monitor their perceived exertion and become more proficient at lowering and raising cardiovascular and respiratory effort to fit a prolonged exercise bout (lasting between about 5 to 15 minutes). In addition, teachers should be aware that motivation is a huge factor regarding student participation in cardiovascular activity. The typical elementary school student will receive adequate cardiovascular exercise from participation in games and dances that require a great deal of locomotor movement.

## Muscular Strength & Muscular Endurance

As the result of an exercise program, preadolescent children do not gain strength through an increase in the size of muscular tissue, instead children gain strength through adaptive changes in the neurological system in response to an appropriate regular exercise program. Muscular strength/endurance improvements are specific to the muscles worked. That is, resistance training focusing on the biceps muscles will result in improvements in biceps strength/endurance. In addition, resistance training raises basil metabolic rate, therefore increasing caloric expenditure.

Guidelines for improving muscular strength/endurance include the following:

- Provide resistance to a specific muscle group to the extent that the child can do several repetitions of an activity, but become fatigued by the last repetition. Resistance bands, light weights, or activities requiring the child to move his/her own body weight are acceptable.
- Provide activities, which work several muscle groups (e.g., upper body, lower body, back, and abdominal area).
- Allowing for a day of rest of the particular muscle group worked may be optimal.
- Remember that lactic acid is a by-product of this type of activity and may cause some muscle soreness in older children.
- Isotonic exercises or "free weight" type activities work the muscle harder at certain angles of rotation and less hard at other angles. Although this type of activity may be fun and motivational to students, it needs to be very closely monitored so those students do not experience trauma that may damage their bones. This includes never letting students lift amounts of weight that are uncomfortable, or with which that they cannot perform several repetitions with good form. In addition young children should never be allowed to lift uncomfortable amounts of weight over their heads.
- Isokinetic exercises provide optimal resistance throughout the entire range of motion at a joint. This type of activity is primarily permitted through exercise "machines." These devices are acceptable, but should be fitted to accommodate the size each individual student. Weight machines are available trough a variety of vendors.
- Isometric exercises include resistance with no movement of the muscle being worked. For example, pushing against the wall. There is no real practical use for this type training in a physical education setting, as strength gains are primarily limited to the specific angle of the contraction.
- Progression- It is important to start easy and progress slowly. Starting students with to difficult a program can be extremely discouraging.

<u>Practical Implication</u>

While regular active participation in a variety of games, dances, and skill development activities is probably adequate for the development of muscular strength/endurance and the development of bones, resistance exercises can also be motivating to some children. In addition, obese children, who are often not the top performers in activities requiring a great deal of movement, might experience more success in resistance-type activities. This feeling of accomplishment and success may help these students to develop a better self-concept. This feeling of adequacy in the physical domain may increase their desire to participate in physical activity during class as well as during times of free play with peers.

## **Flexibility**

Increasing the range of motion at a joint can improve performance of physical activities such as throwing, kicking, and running. In addition an optimal range of motion can lesson the likelihood of muscular injury.

Guidelines for improving flexibility include the following:
- Only perform flexibility exercises when the muscles are warm. Muscles can be warmed through a low intensity, cardiovascular exercise.
- Do not engage in ballistic or bouncing activities. It is believed that this bouncing motion may increase flexibility at the expense of micro tears to muscles and possibly other tissues needed for joint stability.
- Only bend a joint in the direction that it is designed (biomechanically) to bend. Twisting or "torking" skeletal articulations can cause damage to ligaments and other structures that, over time, may compromise joint stability.
- Static stretching is approved as an appropriate method to increase the elasticity of muscle.

## **Body Composition**

Aerobic activity of significant duration will utilize fat directly as part of the metabolic process involved in providing energy for prolonged exercise. Resistance training will tone muscle, and increase metabolism thus increasing caloric expenditure.

# Guidelines for Creating a Positive Attitude toward Physical Fitness

- Physical Education teachers should be good role models in staying physically fit, themselves.
- Parental involvement should be encouraged.
- Students and their parents should be made aware of the importance of health-related fitness during the childhood years, and the diseases associated with a sedentary lifestyle.
- Embarrassment should be avoided.
- Pre-established long-term and short-term goals should be individualized.
- Activities should be motivating to students.
- A wide variety of fitness activities should be offered.
- A well planned physical fitness program should be implemented on a daily basis.
- Fitness activities outside of class time should be an integral part of the program.

# Chapter 7
# Developing Curriculum and Daily Lessons

*PLAY WITH ME*
*I TRIED TO TEACH MY CHILD WITH BOOKS;*
*HE GAVE ME ONLY PUZZLED LOOKS.*
*I TRIED TO TEACH MY CHILD WITH WORDS;*
*THEY PASSED HIM BY, OFT UNHEARD.*
*DESPAIRINGLY I TURNED ASIDE,*
*"HOW SHALL I TEACH THIS CHILD?" I CRIED*
*INTO MY HANDS HE PUT THE KEY*
*"COME," HE SAID, "PLAY WITH ME."*

**Anonymous**

Curriculum should be developed around a central philosophy of physical education. Once a basic philosophy has been established, content standards and student objectives for each grade level should be determined. Finally, the scope, sequence and balance of instructional units and daily lessons can be established along with appropriate assessment and evaluation criteria. The final step to developing curriculum involves its constant modification for improvement.

## Content

The content addressed in the curriculum should be based upon the state (or district) content standards and benchmarks. These are typically reflections NASPE's National Standards for Physical Education.

## Determine the Scope, Sequence, and Balance

1. Scope-Yearly content of your curriculum. In the elementary and early childhood programs the scope should be very broad, covering as many activities as possible, rather than focusing on in-depth coverage of only a few selected areas.

2. Sequence- The order in which the content will be taught. Following an appropriate activity progression is important in order to optimize the transfer learning, as well as continually challenged students at an appropriate level.
3. Balance- Pre-established program objectives will determine the amount of coverage required in specific content areas.

## Content Placement
### Modified Method

This is a method of content placement in which several different skill themes or activity areas are addresses within the same week. For example, balance activities may be the focus for two consecutive days, followed by two days of manipulative activities, with a movement awareness theme the 5th day.

The modified method is especially recommended for students in the lower grades (k-2), where   building the foundation of motor skills and movement competence is of primary importance. Typically the complexity of the skills covered at this level is low, and the periodic changes in activities are needed in order to keep students motivated to participate.

### Solid Method

Activities are presented for an extended period of time, perhaps all week or more, with the exclusive focus on one content area. This method works well for students who are more highly motivated regarding a particular activity, and is recommended primarily for 3rd to 6th graders (students beginning to "utilize the foundation," and refine fundamental movement skills). While activities selected for the upper elementary grades tend to be more complex, requiring more time and continuity, it is suggested that at least one day a week should be set aside for a different focus. This may be considered as a break or change of pace activity to ensure motivation. This day should include a simple, but fun activity that could be completed in a single class period.

## Considerations for the Yearly Curriculum Outline

- Determine the number of days you actually have class. Most districts have a set number of days per week students will have PE. This information, in conjunction with your content guidelines helps to determine the number of days to reserve for each selected content theme.

- For elementary students, reserve the first week for the development of classroom management skills and the inevitable constant interruptions that occur at the beginning of the school year.
- Plan time for assessment.
- Plan for rainy days.

## Developing Objectives

1. Objectives should be measurable.
2. Long-term (yearly), Short-term (instructional unit), and daily objectives should be developed.
3. Objectives should reflect all behavioral domains.
4. Objectives should be written in behavioral terms and should include:
    1. Who ("The students will…").
    2. What (the observable behavior to be performed)
    3. Conditions (What activity will they participate in that will help them attain this objective?)

### Value of Written Objectives

1. Objectives keep the lesson focused for the teacher as well as the student.
2. Objectives provide criteria for assessment.
3. Objectives provide for accountability.
4. Objectives help to keep parents as well as administrators and other faculty aware of the importance of their class.

## The Daily Lesson Plan

The daily lesson plan should include the following components:

- Grade level being taught
- Health-related physical fitness objective(s)
- Skill theme objective(s)
- Description of the "skill development" phase of the lesson. The activity/activities should be reproducible from information contained on lesson plan. This phase of the lesson typically includes teaching and guided practice with quality feedback.
- Description of the enhancement activity in which students get to utilize the skills learned during the skill development phase. Generally contains a game, dance or challenge activity.
- Closure

## Phases of the Daily Lesson

1. *Health-Related Fitness*

   At least one-half to one-third of the lesson should focus on health-related physical fitness. If it is not included in a game or activity, then a systematic method should be used; i.e., MWF Aerobic; TTH muscular strength/endurance and flexibility. This part of the lesson should require very little in terms of psychomotor learning or cognition. The intent is to get students moving, so motivation is critical. Understand, the focus is on enhancing physical development.

2. *Skill Development with Guided Practice*

   Variable practice with a variety of activities is important. Teaching by providing demonstrations and guidance with quality feedback is of vital importance. All students need to be appropriately challenged; this may require the need to accommodate students on an individual basis.

3. *Enhancement Phase*

   This summative activity is generally fun and perhaps competitive. The enhancement activity should allow students to use the skills learned during the skill development phase of the lesson in an enjoyable format.

4. *Closure*

   Review and Feedback. The teacher reviews what the objectives of the lesson were and provides the opportunity for the students to relay what they have learned in a personal and non-threatening format.

## Homework in Physical Education

Quality homework assignments should be given at least once a week. Homework has substantial benefits for physical education (Hart, 2002). The Benefits of home tasks can be classified as direct and indirect.

Direct Benefits
- provides extra practice for a specific skill being learned in class
- increases the time spent in physical activity
- provides a greater opportunity for improvement in health related physical fitness
- provides an opportunity to apply skills/knowledge learned in class in a different environmental context, which may enhance learning

## Indirect Benefits (Perhaps most important!)

- informs parents of what their child is learning in physical education.
- advocates for the program
- informs parents of the importance of physical education
- gets parents involved with their child's learning
- gets parents/family participating in physical activity together which may improve dynamic of family unit
- provides parents with the knowledge necessary to help their child master a skill, become more physically fit, or understand a concept
- educates parents regarding the necessity of daily physical exercise and motor development, and its relationship to academic performance and general quality of life

## Considerations for homework assignments:

- Assignment sheets with parent/guardian signatures should be provided for student accountability purposes.
- Time necessitated for each assignment performed with a parent should not require more than about 10 to 15 minutes.
- All assignment should positively reflect the goals of a quality physical education program.
- Assignments should be developed to be educational for the parents as well as the student.
- Assignments should include an explanation of why a particular topic or activity is important and how it relates to children's overall development.
- Assignments should provide an explanation of skill expectations based on the age-related physical and perceptual developmental level of the child.
- Assignments should provide parents with suggestions on how to help their child practice or learn a particular skill.
- Assignments should be designed to be _fun_ and something that can be enjoyable for the family. Lessons should be structured so that adult family members can (and want to) get involved.
- The assignments should not be too difficult for parents to accomplish!

Developmentally appropriate assignments should be utilized for each skill theme taught. See example assignments in the Appendix.

For more "Quality Home Assignments" contact the author of this text (susan.hart@utb.edu)

# Chapter 8
# Optimizing Instruction

Creating appropriate lessons and optimal practice sessions requires knowledge related to human development as well as an understanding of the basic principals of motor learning. This chapter is designed to provide the physical educator with information valuable to designing an effective lesson format. Basically the information in this chapter helps teachers determine the best *method* of teaching a specific skill or concept.

## Factors that Affect Motor Skill Acquisition

- Readiness – A combination of maturation and experience/practice that is associated with a time that students can more easily acquire a skill or understand a concept. Although "readiness" for a specific activity can be estimated by chronological age, variability related to physiological and neurological development, as well as differences in quality affordances makes individual "readiness" for a specific task very difficult to predict.

- Arousal & Performance- There appears to be an optimal level of arousal for optimal performance. This optimal level is very dependent upon the individual as well as the specific activity being taught. In order to maximize teaching effectiveness, instructors need to establish an environment which facilitates an optimal level of arousal for the lesson/activity.

- Developmental Progression needs to be considered when working with young children. Physical growth as well as neurological progression proceeds in the following directions:

    o Cephalocaudal – head to foot
    o Proximodistal – midline to periphery
    o Gross to Fine – gross motor skills are more easily acquired before the development of fine motor proficiency

- Feedback
    o Intrinsic- Internal feedback such as the information received by the learner in terms of vision, hearing, touch, smell, etc. may not be very reliable during the early stages of learning.

- o Extrinsic- The external information received from an outside source like the teacher, video tape, stopwatch, etc. can be useful as students learn motor skills.
- o Meaningful Feedback – Information pertaining to specific aspects of the skill/ skill being learned. This is also referred to as quality feedback and is very beneficial to learning.
- o Knowledge of Results (KR) - Feedback pertaining to the *outcome* or *product* of the performance.
- o Knowledge of Performance (KP) - Feedback related to the *process* of performing the skill. KP is more important than KR in the beginning phases of learning a new skill.
- o Feedback schedule is important- The more the better is <u>not</u> a correct assumption. Too much feedback can lead to a dependence on feedback. The benefits from quality feedback necessitate practice time.
- o Individualize feedback whenever possible.

- Whole Versus Part- Decisions regarding *how* to teach a specific skill is partially dependent upon the *complexity* and *organization* of the task.
  *Complexity*- number of sequential components
  *Organization*- how integrated the sequential parts are to one another
  Generally it is advisable to initially attempt teaching highly organized complex tasks as a whole. Highly organized complex skills are those that require "flow" of movement, making separation of individual components difficult. Examples include: throwing, batting dribbling a basketball, etc.

- Length and Distribution of Practice Sessions- Consider the age and developmental level of the child in light of fatigue and boredom.

- Blocked Versus Random Practice
  - o *Blocked*- All the trials of one task are completed before moving on to the next task.
  - o *Random*- Multiple tasks are presentations simultaneously or in a mixed order.

It appears that *blocked* practice may be more useful at the beginning stages of learning a skill because rapid improvement typically follows. While this may be motivating to students during the initial stages of learning, *random* practice is associated with better results concerning long-term retention.

Theory: When the same task is practiced over and over it not only becomes boring, but since the same motor program is used over and over, little effort or thinking is required. Students using random practice forget the motor program and have to consciously recreate the solution to be successful.

- Variability of Practice- Refers to varying a specific class of movements (e.g., throwing, striking, etc.) with regard to the parameters of *space, force* and *time, and relationships*. Variable practice is important in that it increases skill performance in variable settings.

    o Spatial variation refers to varying movement patterns.
       Direction of movement including up & down; forward & backward; left & right; zigzag and curved.
    o Force variation refers to the amount of muscular exertion.
       Manipulating objects that range from light & heavy.
    o Time variation refers to the speed at which movements are performed.
       Performing movements from slow to fast, or smooth to jerky.
    o Relationship variation refers to the relationships among objects and people.
       Equipment that ranges from small to large. Working alone or with others.

    Variable practice is much more important in "open" skills in which response parameters are   unpredictable (shortstop position in baseball), and perhaps less important in "closed" skills (place-kicker).

- Transfer of Learning- Dependent upon retention and over learning.

- Progression of Skills - Placing skills to be learned into an appropriate sequence.

- Student Attentiveness- The ability to attenuate to, and process relevant information and disregard irrelevant information.

- Teaching Cues- The ability of students to cognitively understand specific factors related to the skill. Cues must be provided by the teacher, video, etc. (e.g., throwing- step with opposite foot, follow through).

- Instructional Format – Refers to how the students are grouped. It is best to set up guided practice sessions where quality individualized feedback is available to all students.

- Establishment of Objectives and Expected Student Outcomes – These should be provided to students before each instructional unit and reiterated on a regular basis.

- Assessment - Student progress should be provided throughout the instructional unit. Parents should also be provided with regular assessment of their children.

- An Effective Plan for Curriculum Presentation

- Developmentally Appropriate Activities – Create lessons that are motivating and challenging, but allow for the students to be successful the majority of the time.

- Maximize Participation and Minimizing Waiting

- Choose an Effective Teaching Style
  o The *Direct Style* is the most teacher controlled approach. Basically the lesson involves the teacher providing an explanation, and a demonstration of the activity to be covered. The teacher then provides skill development through guided practice.
  o The *Task (Station) Style* involves the teacher setting the lesson objectives and selecting the activities; however, the students are responsible for the pace of the lesson. The students are given a variety of tasks and they are allowed to accomplish them at their own pace. Students move from station to station and rotate after a set amount of time has elapsed. Another form of this format is a more *outcome-based style* in which students are required to master a selected skill before moving on to the next skill. Students move at an individual pace, and are tested when they feel they are ready.

<u>Example of volleyball subtests:</u>
- Bump 10 consecutive balls to a designated target area on the gym wall.
- Set the ball against the wall 10 consecutive times in a designated target area on the gym wall.

One of the major problems with the Task Style is that its basis is with *product oriented* assessment.

o The ***Cooperative Learning*** format requires students work together to accomplish common goals. This type of educational format can teach children to develop social skills and to focus on the importance of group rather than individual success. This teaching method can also be used to foster leadership skills as well as enhance students' abilities in a supporting role.
o The ***Problem-Solving*** format involves the teacher preparing activities or "problems" that may have multiple solutions.

<u>Important Considerations for all Instructional Formats</u>
1. Students are actively involved in the lesson the majority of the time.
2. The lessons are motivating, enjoyable, and challenging.
3. The lessons are developmentally appropriate and individualized so that each student can succeed the majority of the time.
4. Realistic learning objectives are pre-established and provided to the students at the outset of the lesson.
5. Regular assessment is provided and students are held accountable for learning.
6. Teachers are actively involved throughout the entire instructional process.
7. Teachers are good role models, and exhibit enthusiasm throughout the lesson.

# Chapter 9
# Creating and Maintaining an Optimal Learning Environment

## Classroom Management
### The Importance of Classroom Rules of Conduct

In any educational environment, ground rules must be set to ensure each student is afforded a positive learning environment that is free from unnecessary distractions. *Rules* can be created and posted before the first day of class, but consider having the students assist in their development, as this gives students a sense of pride and makes the rules easier to administer. Rules should be general in nature. Each should deal with observable behavior, which eliminates problems associated with teacher judgment. Only the rule itself should be listed, while the meaning should be discussed with the class. The rules should be posted prominently on the wall.

Following is a short list of suggested rules with a brief explanation of the behavior each requires.

- *Enter prepared.* - This can mean wearing appropriate clothing and shoes, looking for the instructor while entering, and finding your spot or area.
- *Respect others.* - Give the instructor full attention, give your classmates your attention when it's their turn to talk or demonstrate, and keep your hands to yourself.
- *Use equipment only when instructed to* – Using equipment without permission is distracting and dangerous.

After presenting and discussing the rules, they should be practiced with students. Enforce rules constantly and consistently.

<u>Consequences</u>

After the rules have been discussed, *consequences* for not following them must be determined. Consequences should be listed and posted near the rules, and discussed after rules have been presented.

- Consequences should be clear and specific, so children will know exactly what will occur if they misbehave.
- Consequences should be applied quickly and consistently to all students.
- Remember that negative consequences are used to teach proper behavior, not to punish.

Identify unacceptable behavior and state briefly why it is unacceptable. "You were talking when I was giving instructions, and others cannot hear," or "If you continue not following the rules, someone might get hurt." This way the child knows exactly why he is being addressed, and what he can do to correct his behavior.

Examples of some consequences might be temporary removal from an activity, a phone call or note to a parent, or, if serious, a referral to the principal – but hopefully class will be so enjoyable it will never get to that point.

Important – after asking for acceptable behavior, be vigilant in looking for it, and immediately enforce it with a "thumbs-up," "good job, Jesse!" or a "high five."

<u>Effective Management Tips</u>
- Make sure the first day is fun and engaging. You want students to leave class confident and excited about what awaits them.
- The best strategy for creating an atmosphere that is controlled and optimal for creative learning is to be prepared. Know the lesson and be comfortable with the skills to be taught.
- Be structured – have a routine for students to follow the second they enter your room or the gym. This allows for a comfortable, organized beginning to each class with a minimum of stress.

## Determine Routines
- how students are supposed to enter teaching area
- where and how they should line up
- what they should do if equipment is located in the area
- what signal a teacher uses to get attention or "freeze" a class
- how to set up and put away equipment
- how students are supposed to exit the area

Most physical education classes are large, and it is important to get all students involved and moving right away. Use floor tape or stickers as markers on the floor of the room or gym, staggered in rows and placed so each student can stand on one with a view of the instructor, and cannot touch or reach another student. This can be done on different sides of the room or in a circular pattern, and with a large number of students. As students enter, it their responsibility to stand on a marker and focus on the instructor. As they enter, have music playing. Lead the students in clapping or stepping to a beat, or maybe move into some aerobics or calisthenics. With this method, students are engaged in activity the minute they enter, the instructor can accomplish fitness goals without any wasted time, and the students have not wasted class time sitting and waiting. From this arrangement, the students can then be addressed for the next activity.

Give positive group and individual feedback constantly and **learn the names of your students and use them.** This will greatly help manage behavior while building confidence and self-esteem.

Give clear and specific instructions.

## Deliver instruction efficiently and effectively

- Instruction should be given in *small doses* focusing on one or two points at a time, 30-45 seconds.
- Alternate *short instructional periods* with *activity requiring movement.*
- *Demonstrate* skill, activity, or route.
- *"When* before *what"* – "when I blow the whistle I want you to..."

## Discipline individually

Avoid negative feedback to an entire group, and **do not** punish or discipline an **entire group** for the misbehaviors of an individual or a few individuals. This will lead to mistrust and resentment of the instructor. In addition, children who have been listening and following rules will not get the instruction they deserve.

Demonstrate and be engaged the entire period-the students need to know that you sincerely value what you teach.

With the Exception of a valid medical condition and doctor's orders, expect 100% involvement.

## Creating a Safe Environment for Activity

Elementary students are typically very enthusiastic when physical movement is involved. For children to stay motivated, they must feel that the environment is safe and comfortable. To this extent teachers need to provide an environment in which students feel psychologically safe as well as physically comfortable.

### Psychological Safety

- Students must feel freedom to try new things without the threat of criticism from their peers or the teacher.
- Bullying should not be tolerated.
- Activities should be provided to ensure student success most of the time.
- Students are sometimes fearful to try specific activities. Teachers should provide support and understanding for these students.

### Physical Safety and Comfort

**Exercising in the Heat**

The following factors contribute to the necessity of being vigilant of heat stress as well as keeping a children well hydrated.

- Many children these days rarely exercise outside when the weather becomes uncomfortably hot. Physiological adaptation to warmer climates takes time and many children will complain about the heat even when the teacher and other children are comfortable. Children can take twice as long to adapt to heat as adults (Bar-Or, 1983).
- Children have a greater body surface area compared to their body mass than adults. This allows for more heat to transfer from the environment to through the body surface (Bar-Or, 1983).
- Children produce more metabolic heat than that produced by adults.
- Children do not sweat as efficiently as adults (Bar-Or, 1983).
- Children have a more difficult time than adults moving heat from the body's core to the surface of the skin. This is a result of a lower cardiac output at a given oxygen uptake compared to adults (Bar-Or, 1983).
- Obese children will feel the effects of heat to a greater extent than their peer.
- Humidity affects the body's ability to cool itself. Heat index charts can be very useful in determining dangerous heat conditions.
- Students with specific disabilities may have more difficulty cooling themselves than their peers.
- Enthusiastic children may not self-monitor their feeling of being overheated until they suffer from some form of heat stress.

# Chapter 10
# Assessment

*Assessment* involves collecting data regarding student performance in some area of interest. Teachers generally use this data to make an *evaluation* about things like fitness level, skill level, student knowledge, etc. In this chapter *assessment* and *evaluation* are discussed in terms of measuring student performance.

Periodic student assessment is an integral component of a quality physical education program because it provides the following functions:
- documents student progress
- enhances student learning
- enhances student motivation
- helps in the selection of appropriate student placement
- provides parents with information about their child
- provides important information needed for program/curriculum development

## What should be assessed?
Assessment should be use to evaluate how well goals and objectives have been accomplished. To the extent that goals and objectives are determined at the time of curriculum development, so is the associated means of assessment and criteria for evaluation. Aspects of a quality curriculum that necessitate periodic evaluation include performance in all three behavioral domains (*cognitive, affective,* and *psychomotor*).

## When should assessment be done?
Assessment should reflect both long-term and short-term goals. Periodic assessment is important to provide both parents and students with information concerning progress. Pre-assessment (before skill or concept is taught) is important in determining a starting point for teaching, as well as determining baseline for comparison (pre-post).

## How should assessment be done?

Two basic forms of assessment should be considered.

*Process-Oriented* assessment provides a measure related to performance or technique. Product-Oriented assessment provides a measure of outcome.

Information regarding process is generally more important, especially in the early stages of learning, than outcome. In other words, the teacher should be more concerned with the form of the overhand throw, than in how many times a target on the wall is hit.

In fact, students who are provided with Product-Oriented goals for psychomotor skills, like throwing a softball, may modify an optimal throwing form in order to improve success at hitting a specified target that may be placed too close to the thrower. This example exemplifies how, often outcome-based criteria, dos not provide a *valid* measure related to skill technique.

## Forms of Evaluation

Student performance may be compared to an appropriate peer group such as in *Norm-Referenced* evaluation. Many physical fitness tests utilize fitness norms. Students scoring in the 95th percentile, for example, can be said to have outperformed 95% of their peers. *Criterion-Referenced* evaluation utilizes a scoring system based on a pre-established degree of excellence.

## Should students receive grades in physical education?

While unfair grading practices can serve to de-motivate students in physical education, many reasons exist for an appropriate grading system especially in the upper-elementary grades.

- Grades are expected in other academic disciplines. A grading system in physical education increases the credibility of the discipline.
- Grades provide a means of accountability for student learning.
- A fair grading system based not only on performance outcomes, but also on individual improvement may tend to motivate students.
- A grading system in physical education provides evidence that goals were pre-established.
- Grades inform parents about provide information to parents.
- Grades communicate a level of proficiency for subsequent physical placement.

## Performance or Improvement?

Students within any grade classification at the elementary level will differ tremendously with regard physical as well as neurological development. This alone, provides enough justification for a grading system which considers individual improvement as a major factor in the determination of grades.

## Considerations for a Fair Grading System in Physical Education

- Good grades should be attainable for all children within the grading period.
- Grading criteria should be explained to the students in plenty of time for them to do well.
- Periodic assessment should happen throughout the learning process.
- Grades should only be based on skills or concepts that you have taught.
- Grading and evaluation should reflect predetermined goals and objectives.
- The type assessment utilized should match the goals. If assessing the form of throwing a softball, product evaluation (how many times the student hit the target) may not be an appropriate method of assessment.

## Assessment Options Appropriate for Elementary Students

- Teacher Observation – involving process as well as product evaluation
- Peer Observation- utilizing a checklist of critical elements of a skill
- Student Journals- subjective accounts of their experiences in physical
- Homework- assignments involving recall of information taught in class
- Event Tasks- Students, individually or in groups develop a dance, solve a problem, etc.
- Portfolios- collection of student work gathered over a period of time

# Popular Norm-Referenced Assessment Instruments

## Psychomotor Skills
- Denver Developmental Screening Test
- Bruininks-Oseretsky Test
- Peabody Developmental Scales
- Test of Gross Motor Development (TGMD)

## Health-Related Physical Fitness
- AAHPERD Physical Best
- Fitnessgram
- Presidential Physical Fitness Award

# Chapter 11
# Legal Issues

Teachers must understand that they are *legally responsible* to for establishing and maintaining a safe environment for students. This includes *foreseeing* hazards and taking measures to prevent accidents from happening, as well as performing their duties in a reasonable and prudent manner.

A teacher can be held *liable* if a child is injured as a result of his/her *negligence*. The following four major points must be established to determine teacher negligence:

1. *Duty* - Refers to a standard of care that other members within the teaching profession would consider "reasonable."

2. *Breach of Duty* - After it has been established that a particular standard of care was required, it must be proven that such a level of care was <u>not</u> provided. Duty can be breached in two different ways:

   - The teacher can do something that created an unsafe situation. *For example: turned the hose on a slick sidewalk so students could slide around in bare feet.*
   - The teacher did <u>not</u> do something that should have been done. *For example: failed to take care of a broken piece of equipment.*

3. *Injury/Damages* - Physical injury, emotional injury, or financial damages must be proven for liability to be established. Further, it must be proved that the injured part is entitled to compensation as a result of the damages.

4. *Proximate Cause* - It must be shown that the injury or damages occurred as a <u>direct</u> result of the teacher's failure to provide a reasonable standard of care (breach of duty).

## Types of Negligence

- **Malfeasance**- Referred to as an act of *commission*. The teacher *committed* an act that was unlawful and wrongful.

   *Example: The teacher has a student go across the street to a friend's house during physical education class time to pick up a piece of equipment. While there he/she experiences an accident with an injury.*

- **Misfeasance**- Occurs when a teacher makes a *mistake*. The teacher follows proper procedures but does not perform according to the required standard of conduct.
   *Example: The teacher shows up to recess duty, but allows too many children on a piece of playground equipment. The equipment breaks causing a student to experience an injury.*

- **Nonfeasance**- Referred to as an act of *omission*. The teacher *omitted* his/her duty. This type of negligence is determined by a teacher <u>not</u> carrying out a required duty. In this situation, the teacher is aware of proper procedures, but does not follow them.
   *Example: The teacher knows he/she should monitor students in the gym, but fails to do so.*

- **Contributory Negligence**- May be determined if the injured party is determined to be partially responsible for the injury. While this form of negligence would never be determined in situations involving kindergarten or even first graders, children in the upper elementary grades are expected to exercise reasonable judgment and to follow basic directions. The maturity level of the child, as well as the child's ability, and experience is considered when determining contributory negligence.

   *Example: With the door shut but unlocked, a 5th grade student sneaks into the equipment room and hurts himself/herself with a piece of equipment.*

# Guidelines for Preventing Student Injury and Legal Issues

1. Create daily lesson plans for each class and follow them.
2. Insure safe equipment, and include the equipment used in your lesson plans.
3. If in doubt of any procedure, or activity consult your administrator.
4. Make sure all activities are developmentally appropriate for each individual child.
5. Students that are afraid of performing a particular activity may be gently encouraged, but it is also wise to give them a second choice of activities.
6. "No participation" notes from home mean <u>no participation</u> in any physical activity, even if the student wants to participate.
7. Emergency first aid equipment should be readily available and the teacher should know how to use it.
8. In case of an accident, the first responsibility of the teacher is to render first aid.
9. Eliminate or secure equipment that may be an "attractive nuisance."
10. Take care not to mismatch students of different size or abilities.
11. Post an emergency plan that has been approved by your school administrator.
12. Fill out all paperwork including incident/accident report forms when situations occur.

Liability Insurance is suggested for <u>all</u> teachers. Do not assume that your school district has purchased insurance for you.

# References

Bar-Or, O. (1983). *Pediatric sports medicine for the practitioner.* New York: Springer-Verlag.

Bar-Or,O., and Rowland, T.W. (2004). *Pediatric exercise medicine.* Champaign, Ill: Human Kinetics.

Gabbard, C. (1994). *Physical Education for Children.* New Jersey: Prentice-Hall.

James, W. (1890). *The principles of Psychology.* New York: Dover.

Magill, R. A. (2001). *Motor learning: Concepts and application.* 6th ed. Dubuque, IA: Wm. C. Brown.

National Association for Sport and Physical Education. (2004). *Moving into the future: National standards for physical education* (2nd ed.). Reston, VA: Author.

Piaget, J. (1952). *The origins of intelligence in children.* New York: International University Press.

Piaget, J. (1963). *The origins of intelligence in children.* (M. Cook, Trans.). New York: W.W. Norton & Co., Inc.

Piaget, J. (1985). *The equilibrium of cognitive structures: The central problem of intellectual development.* Chicago: University of Chicago Press.

Pinhas-Harniel, O. (1996). *Increase incidence of non-insulin-dependent diabetes mellitus among adolescents.* The Journal of Pediatric Exercise Medicine.

Schmidt, R. A. (1988). *Motor control and learning.* 2nd ed. Champaign, Ill: Human Kinetics.

U.S. Department of Health and Human Services. (1996). *Physical activity and health: A report of the Surgeon General.* Atlanta, GA: Center for Disease Control and Prevention.

# Appendix

# Powerwalking/Flexibility Assignment

## Student Instructions

1. Teach your exercise partner how to powerwalk.
2. Explain to your partner 3 ways that powerwalking is good for your body.
3. Do a "warm up" walk for 2 minutes and explain to your partner the importance    of warming up before exercise.
4. Powerwalk with your partner for 10 minutes.
5. After walking, perform 3 flexibility exercises for your legs, 2 for your arms, and 1 for your back.
6. Explain to your partner the benefits of flexibility, and why it is best to perform flexibility exercises after your muscles have warmed up.
7. Shake hands and tell your partner "thank you."

# Parent Information Sheet

**Powerwalking** is an excellent activity for developing cardiovascular endurance as well as muscular endurance and strength. Based on your child's age he/she is developmentally capable of performing this activity for the amount of time required for this assignment. His/her level of fitness, as well as your level of fitness, may require that the intensity of the exercise be modified so that you can finish the activity together.

*Cardiovascular* exercise, includes "aerobic" activities that last for several minutes and require elevated breathing and heart rates. For an optimal workout adults should perform "aerobic" activities which last for at least 20 minutes several times a week. Children are motivated by shorter bouts of this activity, but should engage in this form of exercise on all or most days of the week.

## Importance of Aerobic Activities for Young Children
- Research suggests that without regular and appropriate aerobic activity during childhood, the lungs, the heart, and the vasculature might not develop to their full potential, even if kids start to "work out" when they're teen-agers.
- Aerobic activities help a child's body to utilize the foods they eat.
- Aerobic activities help the body to circulate oxygen and nutrients to the brain which helps children to concentrate.
- Research indicates that most children, regardless of their fitness level, perform better in school when they get daily aerobic exercise.
- Cardiovascular activities help children to maintain a healthy body weight, and to look good which increases their self-confidence and self-esteem.
- Cardiovascular fitness is a vital component to all physical activities. Thus, fit kid tends to participate more in other physical activities.

# Student Assignment Sheet (Powerwalking)

Explain 3 ways that powerwalking is good for your body.

1._____

2._____

3._____

List 3 muscle groups which are very active during powerwalking.

1._____

2._____

3._____

List 2 benefits of being flexible

1._____

2._____

Explain why it is important to do flexibility exercises after your muscles have been warmed up.

_____

_____

# Parent Sign-Off

My child _____ completed the checked items below pertaining to
         (child's name)
the powerwalking assignment.


_____ Powerwalked for 10 minutes with a parent/guardian.


_____ After walking they performed the flexibility exercises with their
parent/guardian.


_____ Shook hands with their walking partner and said "thank you."



Parent's/Guardian's Signature _____

# Throw/Catch
# Assignment

## Student Instructions

- Using a bean bag, tennis ball or ball of similar size, teach your partner the proper arm and leg motion for throwing overhand.
- Teach your partner how to catch the ball using both hands. Remind your partner to have "soft hands" as he/she catches the ball.
- Play catch for at least 10 minutes. Remember you must retrieve the ball regardless of who missed it!
- Tell your partner "Thank You" and shake his/her hand.

# Parent Information Sheet

## Throwing

One of the basic motor skills covered in a quality physical education curriculum is *underhand* and *overhand* throwing. Throwing is a manipulative skill that requires a great deal of body control through a sequence of movements. This homework assignment is designed to provide extra practice for your child as he/she learns the *overhand* throw.

From a developmental perspective, your child is capable of becoming quite proficient at this skill, but it requires a great deal of practice.

## Catching

We have also been working on catching in physical education class. Catching requires visual perception capabilities that, in many 2nd grade children have not quite reached adult levels in terms of development. The ability to track a moving object is often limited by an immature level of dynamic vision (the ability to discriminate certain aspects of moving objects). Children also have limited peripheral vision (compared to adults). In this case we are talking about vertical peripheral vision, such that, if you are standing close to your child and excessively arc the ball, visual tracking becomes more difficult because the child must now tilt their head in order to keep it in site. In addition, the complicated series of perceptual judgments required to coincident time specific movements of the body and hands in order to catch a moving object can often be quite difficult for young children.

The key is to be patient, and to understand that children develop at different rates according to a genetic timetable. That is, based on developmental physiology (not just practice) some children will develop the ability to track moving objects sooner than other children. Children having a difficult time tracking the ball should never be compared to children with a developmental advantage as this can be very discouraging. Create practice sessions which are appropriate for your individual child. Your child should be challenged, but successful most of the time.

# Parent Guide to Teaching

Here are some teaching suggestions that you might find helpful as you work with your child:

## Throwing

- Stand facing the target at a slight angle, with the non-throwing side facing the target.
- Position body weight on throwing hand side.
- Point elbow (non-throwing arm) at the target, while holding the ball just above, but slightly away from, the throwing side ear.
- While stepping toward the target with the non-throwing side leg, twist your pointed elbow away with a hard twist of the trunk, and throw the ball at the target.

## Catching

- Stand with feet slightly apart facing the incoming ball.
- Hold hands relaxed and in front of the body with the elbows slightly bent.
- The eyes should follow the flight of the ball into the hands.
- Hands and arms should give upon contact with the ball, and weight should shift from front to back.
- Throw the ball softly at you child without excessive arcing (throwing it too high). Stand at a distance so that your child is successful most of the time. Move farther away as ability permits.

# Student Assignment Sheet (Throw/Catch)

## Skill: Overhand Throw

1. Which arm do you use to throw the ball? _____

2. What does the arm without the ball do during the throwing motion?
   _____

3. Which leg do you step forward with as you throw the ball? _____

4. Why is it important that you twist your body when you throw overhand?
   _____

5. List 3 muscle groups used in overhand throwing.
   1. _____
   2. _____
   3. _____

## Skill: Catching

1. Explain what is meant by "soft hands."
   _____

2. Explain the position of your hands as you wait for the ball.
   _____

3. Explain the position of your legs as you wait for the ball.
   _____

4. Why is important for you to offer to get the ball whenever it is missed?
   _____

## Parent Sign-Off

My child _____ completed the checked items below
　　　　　　　(child's name)
pertaining to the throw/catch assignment.


_____ Played catch with parent/guardian for at least 10 consecutive minutes.


_____ Explained the appropriate position of the arms and legs prior to and during the throwing motion.


_____ Demonstrated good sportsmanship and offered to retrieve the ball when it was missed.



Parent's/Guardian's Signature _____